Cook Memorial Public Library

3 1122 01201 1396

JUL 1 4 2011

S0-BDM-973

ANIMAL FAMILIES / FAMILIAS DE ANIMALES

DOLPHINS / DELFINES
LIFE IN THE POD / VIDA EN LA MANADA

Willow Clark Traducción al español: Eduardo Alamán

PowerKiDS
press
New York

COOK MEMORIAL LIBRARY
413 N. MILWAUKEE AVE.
LIBERTYVILLE, ILLINOIS 60048

Published in 2011 by The Rosen Publishing Group, Inc.
29 East 21st Street, New York, NY 10010

Copyright © 2011 by The Rosen Publishing Group, Inc.

All rights reserved. No part of this book may be reproduced in any form without permission in writing from the publisher, except by a reviewer.

First Edition

Editor: Jennifer Way
Book Design: Julio Gil

Traducción al español: Eduardo Alamán

Photo Credits: Cover, pp. 4–5, 9, 15 (right), 19, 21, 23, 24 (top left, bottom) iStockphoto/Thinkstock; back cover © www.iStockphoto.com/Alexey Bannykh; pp. 7, 11 (top), 13, 24 (top right) Comstock/Thinkstock; pp. 11 (bottom), 14–15 (main, left) Shutterstock.com; p. 17 David J. Slater/Getty Images.

Library of Congress Cataloging-in-Publication Data

Clark, Willow.
  [Dolphins. Spanish & English]
  Dolphins = Delfines : life in the pod : vida en la manada / by Willow Clark. — 1st ed.
      p. cm. — (Animal families = Familias de animales)
  Includes index.
  ISBN 978-1-4488-3126-5 (library binding)
  1. Dolphins—Juvenile literature. 2. Familial behavior in animals—Juvenile literature. I. Title. II. Title:
Delfines.
  QL737.C432C5518 2011
  599.53—dc22
                                     2010025809

Manufactured in the United States of America

CPSIA Compliance Information: Batch #WW11PK: For Further Information contact Rosen Publishing, New York, New York at 1-800-237-9932

Web Sites: Due to the changing nature of Internet links, PowerKids Press has developed an online list of Web sites related to the subject of this book. This site is updated regularly. Please use this link to access the list: www.powerkidslinks.com/afam/dolphin/

CONTENTS

CONTENIDO

Dolphins live in groups, called **pods**.

Los delfines viven en grupos llamados **manadas**.

A pod can have any number of dolphins. Some pods have hundreds of dolphins.

Las manadas pueden tener diferente número de delfines. Algunas llegan a tener cientos de delfines.

Dolphins breathe air through **blowholes** at the tops of their heads.

Los delfines respiran a través de **orificios nasales** en la parte superior de su cabeza.

Blowhole
—————
Orificio nasal

Spotted dolphins and spinner dolphins are two kinds of dolphins.

El delfín manchado del Atlántico y el delfín girador son dos tipos de delfines.

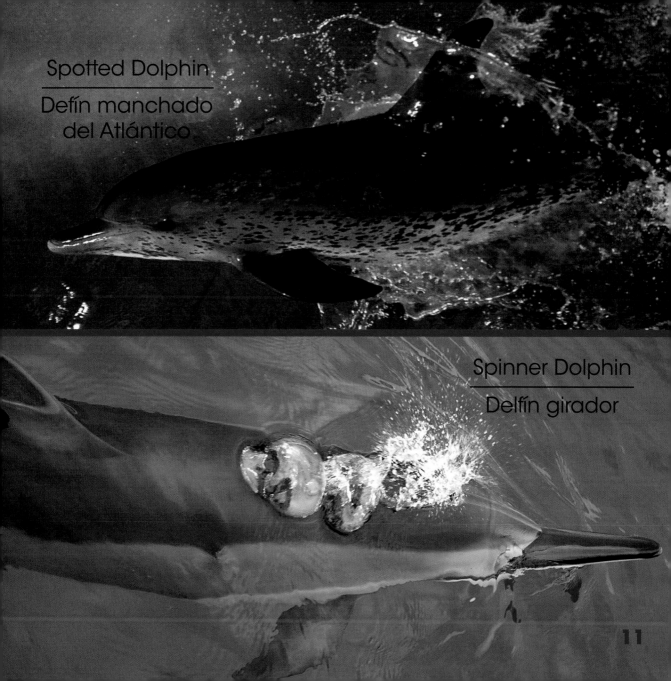

Spotted Dolphin

Defín manchado
del Atlántico

Spinner Dolphin

Delfín girador

11

Dolphins make sounds to talk to other dolphins.

Los delfines producen sonidos para comunicarse con otros delfines.

The pod works together to hunt for food. Dolphins eat fish, squid, and shrimp.

La manada trabaja junta para conseguir comida. Los delfines comen peces, calamares y camarones.

Shrimp
—
Camarón

Fish
—
Peces

15

When a dolphin finds fish to eat, it makes sounds to tell the rest of the pod.

Cuando un delfín encuentra comida, hace un ruido para avisar al resto de la manada.

The pod works together when a member is hurt. The pod helps it come up for air.

Cuando un miembro de la manada está herido, el resto de la manada acude en su ayuda.

Baby dolphins are called **calves**. The mother dolphin helps her calf learn to swim.

Las mamás delfín ayudan a sus **bebés** a aprender a nadar.

Calves stay with their
mothers when they
are young.

De pequeños, los bebés
delfín se quedan con
sus madres.

Words to Know / Palabras que debes saber

blowhole / (el) orificio nasal

calf / (el) bebé delfín

pod / (la) manada